SECRETS OF A COMPLEX LIFE

JIGNESH AHALGAMA

Notion Press Media Pvt Ltd

No. 50, Chettiyar Agaram Main Road,
Vanagaram, Chennai, Tamil Nadu – 600 095

First Published by Notion Press 2022
Copyright © Jignesh Ahalgama 2022
All Rights Reserved.

ISBN 979-8-88530-323-1

To my son, Pinank, my daily reminder of All the happiness in my Life.

Bless you.

Contents

Contents

Acknowledgements

My son Pinank and My nephew Shivam, are my bundle of happiness. Always reminding me to be happy. Thanks to them and their smiles I have been able to get through anything that came my way.

I would like to thank my family members who stood by me and chose to undertake this journey with me. My wife-Sonal, my parents, my brother-Ashwin, and Sister-in-law Nayana. Thank you for being there for me, supporting me and picking me up even in times I had lost hope.

A big thank you to my closest friends, Piyush Lakhani, Girish Karamcheti and Kirtan Vamanjur for inspiring and supporting me to publish my learnings in the form of a book. Without their encouragement I would never have been brave enough to accomplish this.

A special thanks to Mridhula Vamanjur for reviewing the book and giving her feedback. Her feedback helped me understand a reader's perspective of the book before it went onto shelves

I would also like to thank the following friends and colleagues who have now become a steady part of my life—Anubhav Nagal, Datta Nimekar, Gokul Chandra, Irfan Babla, Dr. Nandkishore Yadav, Praveen Srivastva, Dr. Rahul Dabre, Rinkesh Goyani, Rinku Lakhani, Rupesh Atnure, Ravi Soni, Sumathi, Sabir Syed, Sandeep Markhelkar, Sireesha, Tanvi Vaghela, Dr. Vinay Patil and all my dear and near friends whose names I forgot to mention here—for always trusting and encouraging me to write more about happiness and success.

A special thanks to the strange young lady I never got the name of, for positively changing my entire life. This book is in place because she inspired my positive thinking.

I would finally like to thank my editor, Ananya Azad, without whom this book would never be complete. Thank you for helping me give life to my thoughts.

Lastly, I would like to thank my dear readers for believing in me and my discoveries about life, happiness and success.

My Inspiration

Leading by example is one of the most powerful tools one can use to inculcate a positive change in others. So, I have decided to share my personal experience and my inspiration to write this book.

I come from the field of science. All my life, I have depended on scientific explanations alone. How could someone ever change their life by just thinking? For me, life was always very simple and raw hard work was the only key to results. But one day, almost like an epiphany, my whole perspective changed. My perception of happiness, positive thinking, success and life in itself, all changed for the better.

Everyone asked me the reason for this conversion of ideas. "What happened to you?" "How did this happen?" Some impressed, some plain curious.

I always thought of the best way to explain it and that has led me to write this book. If my experience can help even one person—touch even one soul—it would make the world a little happier and isn't that all a writer wants? To make an impact.

For me, I used to be a very introverted person, could not possibly initiate a conversation with a stranger for the life of me. And to talk to a girl whom I've never met before, that too on a random journey, felt next to impossible. But to my surprise, this is exactly what happened to me when everything changed.

A famous poem once said, "People come into your life for a reason, a season or a lifetime". Such simple lines, yet more knowledgeable and honest than anything one would ever find.

New people keep coming into our lives in so many different ways. But not all stay back; some just drift away with time, while others leave even before you could get the chance to understand them. But all of these people come in as one of the following:

1) A Reason

2) A Season

3) A Lifetime

1) A reason

They simply come into your life for a particular reason. Maybe to help you through a difficult time, teach you an important lesson, or support you when you most need it. "To aid you physically, emotionally or spiritually."

Almost like a godsend: present when you need them and may leave when you no longer do. That's just how it is, whether you want them to stay or not. So accept it, thank them and move on because their work is done.

2) A season

These people may come into your life for a longer period. They blossom your life like the monsoon, give you sweet memories like winter and bring in the heat like summer, help you experience peace, love, pain and growth, but eventually they too leave, just like any season would. So, you should understand them, thank them, and accept it like you would accept and enjoy the different seasons of the year.

3) A lifetime

These people come into your life to stay. Whatever the situation may be, they teach you the most important lessons and create bonds that last a lifetime. Identify them, respect them and thank them for coming into your life. They are the ones who will never leave.

Now, I am going to tell you about a person who came into my life for a reason. Remember how I mentioned a girl who changed my entire perception of life? Yes, it was this very young lady around 25-27 years of age, whom I met on a short flight from

Ahmedabad back to Hyderabad. As I have already mentioned I used to be an introvert, keeping to myself and minding my own business. But this lady was different, her face radiated confidence, spirituality and motivation. It is something one can barely explain. She took the initiative to start a conversation with me and I was caught off guard with all the knowledge she had gained, for someone so young. I was so impressed by her personality that I dared to get out of my comfort zone and ask her to share her secret. The one that made her who she was.

As confident as she was, she did not hesitate to share her thoughts and ideas with me. She was assertive in her words and her ways and believed that everyone could lead an optimal life and be successful. This got me wondering how one; that is, I, could implement such a lifestyle.

I hadn't ever considered the need for a change before so I just didn't know where to start and asked her to guide me a little.

To start things off, she asked me to do these three things every day:

1. Wake up early every day. Ideally around the same time

2. Practice some form of meditation and exercise, even if it is only for 15minutes

3. Read any book for a minimum of 30 minutes per day.

Still feeling a little lost, I asked her if it would really be sufficient. To this, she smiled and calmly reassured me that it was more than sufficient and that I would eventually understand. In that second, this lady who was way younger than me seemed older and wiser than anybody I had met in a long time. Not that I still completely believed her, but I felt that there was no harm in trying.

So I tried implementing suggestions in my daily routine, and truly started to notice the differences;

- Waking up early gave me a head-start every day,

- Exercise helped make my body feel fitter, meditating made me feel more at peace and

- Reading just kept teaching me something new every day

I realized that for so long I had been struggling with the negativity within me and had almost completely stopped seeing the positive side of things. I was lacking in confidence, which had impacted both my personal and professional life and kept hoping for different results while refusing to change my ways. I had never believed in 'life-changing conversations' or 'the power of positive thinking'.

But now, things were different. After implementing the advice given to me by that young lady, I managed to slowly turn all the negatives into positives. I have developed a new power of imagination that helped me see all situations in a new light. Sometimes I observe my growth over this period and appreciate how I have learned to love things and the people around me. It gives me happiness. This power of letting go and forgiving those who have hurt me, for my own sake if not theirs. Frankly, it is a huge weight that has been lifted to a point that I can confidently share anything that comes to my mind without worrying about judgment from the people around me.

To this day, I find it surprising how a chance meeting with a random stranger had such a profound impact on my life.

I wanted to dedicate this book to that young lady and thank her for changing my life.

I can only hope that this book can have a similar effect on anyone who chooses to read it.

Introduction

Happiness and sorrow, success and failure are all part of life, two sides of the same coin. We usually try to find a way to be happy and successful from external sources. When I tried to challenge this traditional way of living, I discovered the three main elements of life; Happiness, Forgiveness and Attachments. It taught me that life is art, the importance of the way we think and of the adversities we face. Of how it all adds value to life and helps us be happy and successful.

My intention to write this book is to increase awareness about all of the above. We tend to think of life as something very complicated when in reality, it is only as complicated as we make it for ourselves. Keeping that in mind, I have put together a series of short stories and analogies, comparing us and our lives to the most basic aspects of it all. In order to simplify things, remove the burden of all the adversities in life, to focus on the power of ones mind and the narratives it can create.

No matter who you are or where you are in life. This book can help you change your life. Everything that happens in your life plays a part in taking you to your final destination, and your final destination is only as appealing as your understanding of it. We all wonder, what would we feel at the time of our death? Will we regret our decisions? Or will we be satisfied? Each situation has two sides; this book will help you discover the positive one.

I have correlated things that stood out throughout my journey to date and put down my understanding of what they say about life itself.

But this isn't about my journey, it's about yours. Philosophy is only as good as it can convey itself, and to make sure of that, I have made every chapter one that can stand alone on its own, giving my readers the chance to reflect on each one separately. The intention is to guide and encourage you to push forwards and towards your own version of a happy and successful life.

The contents of this book are therefore divided into 7 sub-sections to make it easier to navigate.

1. Elements of life – This includes the 3 major elements that play an important role throughout our journeys.

2. Importance of thoughts – This section focuses on the power of the mind, of your thoughts and perspectives. How they can make and break everything. These chapters, one by one, help you understand your subconscious self, slowly preparing you for the chapters ahead. Once you open yourself up to something, you allow it to make its intended impact. So, what can or cannot impact you, is for you to choose. This section further talks about this and a lot more.

3. Life is an art – The chapters in this section directly compare life to themselves, talking about how life is a creation of art and needs to be treated as one.

4. Let go – This is one standalone chapter focusing on the importance of being strong, especially during hard times. There is no win without a loss.

5. Importance of adversity – It is one thing to ask someone to be strong and another to understand the importance of those hard times. This section talks about pressure, change, obstacles and even depression. A way to emphasize on and empathize with pain.

6. Find the solution – There is no point in addressing a problem if you cannot present a solution. This section, in its way, offers advice for the same. Emphasizing patience and hard work and our ability to work through everything.

7. The Balance sheet – This is the last chapter of the book. It is as self-explanatory as its name. It gives you a chance to summarize everything that you have read till now and review your experience. There is no better way to conclude a journey than journaling the results, is there?

Elements of Life

Chapter 1: Happiness

"Happiness is not something readymade.
It comes from your own actions"

– Dalai Lama

Everyone wants to be happy in their lives. But what is happiness? Does anyone know what it actually means?

Happiness is a relative term. To be happy, you have to know to suffer, else how can you know that you are actually happy?

We tend to believe that happiness comes from external things, like:

People

Things

Places

You may have a goal in your life which you believe, once achieved, will bring you happiness. It may be:

- Finding someone to love

- Buying your own house

- Or even going on a world tour

Close your eyes and think about what would make you happy. This list could be never-ending.

Once you acquire these goals you realize, the satisfaction they bring is only momentary, you then create another goal that you believe might finally land at everlasting happiness and so on. Unfortunately, the happiness you derive from these achievements is only temporary. You see, happiness is not an object that can be bought or acquired.

True happiness isn't the surface level burst of feelings you feel when something good happens but the state of being content with your reality and the ability to move forward with change. It is something that can stay with you forever.

To get this state of happiness you have to work towards self-mastery. It is a journey from outward to inward; which requires spiritual growth and empowering thoughts over limiting ones. I further talk about this in the coming chapters but for now, here are a few steps that could help.

How to cultivate self-mastery?

- Live in the present moment; how do you live in the present moment?

  ➢ Start each day with a smile

- ➢ Be thankful for what you have

- ➢ Pay attention to every small thing around you

- ➢ Stop living in the past or for the future— one is gone and the other hasn't even arrived yet.

- Realize the power the Present holds. It is the only reality that matters.

- Make your mind and body fit

  - ➢ Meditate- It will empower your thoughts

  - ➢ Read- it will empower your thinking

  - ➢ Exercise- It will make your body fit

- Enjoy and celebrate each small success of yours and others

- Let go of all the things which give you suffering- Nothing is permanent and not every fight is worth fighting for. Prioritize.

- Keep a journal and review your goals and actions so you can always keep track of your progress

What makes you happy?

Chapter 2: Forgiveness

"True forgiveness is when you can say, "Thank you for that experience."

– Oprah Winfrey

Life is too short and filled with innumerable uncertainties. One may never know what is to happen in the very next moment. What we do know, is that we all make mistakes. A lot of times, under certain circumstances, we end up hurting and wronging others, be it mere strangers or the one's dearest to us. But that doesn't make us evil or unworthy as people, does it? We are all humans here and none of us is perfect. We all end up facing the consequences of our actions one way or another. That doesn't make us any less worthy of happiness.

We are all learning from our mistakes, working on ourselves, for ourselves, every single day. Yet, we find it so hard to forgive each other. Why are we fighting? Instead of accepting each other's faults, we blame and torment each other. Isolating those who most need help and ourselves from the ones who can help aid us.

When we make a mistake, we pray to God for forgiveness. If we can expect redemption from God, then why can't we forgive others?

Forgiveness is a vital element for a happy life. It is what makes us kind and life easier for all.

Not so long ago, a dear friend of mine told me his story; which I will now share with you. A story of a mere quarrel that happened between two friends. A fight that was a product of circumstances and mistakes that were soon realized by both parties. Unfortunately, fueled by their ego and stubbornness, both the friends kept waiting for the other to come and talk to them. This went on till one sudden day, one friend got into a car accident and passed away. Ever since my dear friend's life filled with regret for not forgiving his friend. Holding on to his ego, only to lose someone so dear to him and all because of a misunderstanding that could have been solved in a moment.

I am sure my reader, that we all understand the pain of regret.

If we choose to forgive somebody, it will not change the past. But it will change the present, and our future. Forgiveness has nothing to do with others; it is for the ones who have been wronged to move forward. When we let go, we feel the lightness in our hearts. A healing power for the soul.

Forgiving your wrongdoers is not being the "bigger man", it is freeing yourself from the pain of their actions.

It is very difficult to live with regret. So, forgive those who have hurt you, considering any moment could be our last. Don't keep anything for tomorrow. Leave your ego behind, apologize to the ones whom you have wronged and forgive the way you would want to be forgiven. We are here to live and spread the fragrance of love and happiness.

Talk about three people you want to but haven't yet been able to forgive.

1) ____

2) ____

3) ____

Chapter 3: Attachment

*"Attachment is the source of
all suffering. To be free from
suffering, free yourself
from attachments"*

– Buddha

Attachment is a feeling of a bond created with someone or something over a shared period of time. In your life, you may feel attached to people, places, set of beliefs, or occasions. Notice that you usually tend to only feel attached to things from your past. Have you ever really had an attachment to the present moment? Probably not. This is because we have guided and trained our minds to ignore the uncertainty of the present moment and safeguard ourselves within the blanket of our memories and past experiences. Below are some examples showing how you are stuck in your past.

- You cannot stop thinking about the last place you worked at or lived in; because you made such good memories there.

- You always compare the people coming into your life with the loved ones who are now far away or no longer there.

- You tend to revisit occasions and events from previous years in your head, unconsciously and unfairly comparing them to your present moments.

- When things get hard, you end up reassessing your older beliefs even though you actively let go of them. Simply for the sake of familiarity and comfort.

Remember that your outer world is a reflection of your inner thoughts. Ultimately you are telling your subconscious mind that the person, that place, that occasion or belief was way better than where you are right now. Your subconscious mind is the captain of your life; it will immediately react to your command and make that feeling come true.

Whatever those people, places, occasions or beliefs were, they existed in the past; they are no longer your reality. You just cannot recreate those moments again. You can only recreate the memories, but will those memories give you the same kind of happiness? No matter how good or bad a moment may be, the effects of its memories will eventually fade away with time. You need to free yourself from such attachments to open the doors to happiness and success.

Simple steps to break free from fruitless attachments:

- Educate yourself about your life and try to love everything around you.

- Embrace and accept all the people coming your way in every stage of life.

- Do not be afraid to be alone and do not depend on anyone for your happiness, be it your own best friend, remember that you are the only companion you really need.

- Do not rely on anybody else to reach your goals, you are the centre of your universe; Believe that you have all the power you seek within you.

- Celebrate and appreciate every event in life like it were your last.

- Live in the present moment.

Make an attachment with your present moment, your life will be beautiful. Your past can't keep you happy all the time, but your present just might.

Do you have any attachment with any person, place or belief? Write down how it is impacting your current life?

Importance of Thoughts

Chapter 4: The Website

"Everyone and everything that shows up in our life is a reflection of something that is happening inside of us."

– Alan Cohen

As you know, I am from the pharmaceutical industry. I have been in the field for about 8 years now. Given my experience, one day I decided to create a startup of my own. It was just a running idea but I decided to meet with a website designer anyway. I eventually found a good web designer and met up with him. He showed me all the different websites he had been working on and I found his work extremely impressive—creative, attractive and substantially informative to say the least. It got me very curious about his process and I requested him to show me how he did it. He then went on to open a file that contained different codes, then he made some changes in those codes and went back to the website we had been previously looking at. It was just a small change in the codes, but now the website looked quite different than before; like it wasn't as attractive anymore; a lot of the functions and parts of the original format were gone. He explained to me how the web page that everybody could see was completely dependent on the codes typed into its file. Therefore, the final product is purely based on the designer or developers coding skills. Making coding is the fundamental aspect of web designing.

That day I drew a parallel that showed me exactly what we are. We are a website.

Sounds absurd, I know. But if you really think about it, we all are just different websites with multiple web pages, all depending on the codes put into them. These codes are different aspects of our life; our thoughts, our ideas and all the information fed to us. Our different web pages react to these codes, turning it all into the final product that is—our personality as displayed to the world.

Now, we may not have control over all the codes put into our system, but with time and experience, we can learn the skill of editing through these codes that exist, learning new ones and being able to filter out the unwanted ones. Making our website as attractive and functional as we would like.

Remember that whatever you do on the inside, will reflect on the outside. If you choose to code with positive thoughts and functional ideas, your website will be beautiful and highly functional. If you choose to keep the negative and disruptive codes, that too will reflect on your website. You can always rewrite the codes by editing out the defects and adding new features. You can make it as colourful as you want and as authentic, as you please.

Nobody can see the codes in your system, all they see is the final product and judge you based on that. Only you know and understand what goes into the process and hence are the only right judge of what your website needs to be like.

So, my reader, every code is important. You can edit out what you don't like and add what you do. Be what you want to be and design your own unique website. And you will never have to doubt yourself again.

"Our outer world is direct reflection of our inner thoughts"

"Nothing in the world gives happiness or troubles you as much as your thoughts. Your thoughts define you and your future. Build your future by nourishing your good thoughts"

Which codes do you think are required to make a webpage of happiness?

Chapter 5: 250

"Affirmations are our mental vitamins, providing the supplementary positive thoughts we need to balance the barrage of negative events and thoughts we experience daily."

– Tia Walker

There is a phrase by Napoleon hill "you have the power to create anything you can imagine. Act on the ideas produced by imagination… You will achieve success."

I started to believe in this phrase when I read '*The secret*' written by Rhonda Byrne. He beautifully described the power of imagination and daily affirmation.

Everything is possible if you have the desire to achieve it. Desire; alongside a positive attitude, intention and proper action towards it.

Do you know how it works? Let me explain in-depth. We have two minds; one is conscious and another is subconscious. Your subconscious mind is powerful and it makes up around 95% of your brainpower. It is a very strange thing when you think about it. It neither is creative nor understands jokes. Yet, it can remember everything you have done, said or witnessed. The remaining 5% of your brain is the conscious mind and has the sole purpose of interacting with the physical world, it can only register, remember and retain a small percentage of everything that you truly are and know. Whatever you actively think and imagine in your conscious mind becomes stronger and more tangible in your subconscious mind. Therefore, whenever you think of something daily—visualize or imagine it, your subconscious mind starts gathering energy from the universe to make it happen. It could be positive or negative. This is called manifesting something using daily affirmations.

The very first time I read *'The Secret'*, I was just graduating. Around this time, I was also preparing for a competitive exam. I was very inspired and started imagining the results with the scorecard with an All India Rank of 250 on it. That was one of the top ranks and I really wanted it. Every day, before I slept and after I woke up, I religiously visualized the scorecard and went on to do my best to achieve that very result. There cannot be any results with plain imagination; it all requires action to make it happen.

Finally, the exam day arrived and I gave my paper. Soon enough, it was also time for the results to come out. I had no expectations to be very honest, but when I looked at the scorecard, it was exactly as I had visualized every day, an All India Rank of 250. I was so overjoyed; I could not believe it myself.

At the time I was still young, and even though I rejoiced in the power of my hard work and belief, I did not really understand the power of those affirmations.

Now that I have come so far—years later, with my changed beliefs—do I truly understand the role it played and how it wasn't just my imagination, but the power of its active assertiveness. Since then, I have been able to use it to help myself way more and I know for sure that you can too.

Steps to manifest your imagination or goals:

1) Make your goal more tangible- Pen down or draw out what you want and put it somewhere you can see it daily.

2) Daily affirmations- Believe in your goal and that you can achieve it, whether you feel good or are feeling low and unworthy; get in front of the mirror and say out loud, "I am the best and I deserve the best. I will make my dreams come true". It may seem strange in the beginning but make it a habit and you will believe it.

3) Make your own affirmations- Start your affirmations with 'I' or 'My' and use a positive tone of words and stick to the present tense.

Avoid words like "I need", "I should", "I want", "I have to" and "I hope".

4) Hype yourself up- Talk about everything you have accomplished, no matter how small and remind yourself that you can do anything you work towards.

5) Believe it when you say it out loud- You cannot manifest your goals if you don't believe in them and yourself.

Your affirmations and imagination will not only help you manifest your dreams but will help you work harder towards them. This will help you maintain a positive outlook in life in general and just like magic; you will start to create your own path to success.

Write down your daily affirmation for your next goal.

Chapter 6: Millet Roti

"Try… Try harder still the taste of mom's made food can't be found in any corner of word"

– Anonymous

Why can't we survive only on restaurant food for a long time? Why does home food feel so much tastier?

Every word and thought has energy. It radiates and impacts the things surrounding you. What is that energy?

I belong to a small village. My parents still live there. Whenever I go to visit, I ask my mother to make me her millet roti for dinner. It tastes so good when she makes it. I can assertively say that it is as perfect as she is. Not even a five-star restaurant can compete with my mother's cooking. At least not for me. And wouldn't you say the same about your own mother? Everybody somehow prefers their mothers cooking to everything else, craves it no matter where in the world they are, over any gourmet restaurant or chef. Have you ever wondered why?

A millet roti only requires 3 ingredients; there is water, flour and salt. The process of cooking it too is very simple, not very time consuming and rather convenient. And yet, there is so much difference in its taste and texture when someone else makes it. It makes me wonder if there is magic in my mother's hands, and if there is, then what is this magic?

Well, it is the intention behind her cooking of course. When a mother cooks for her family, she cooks with love and care, her heart filled with positivity and good wishes for her loved ones. That intention is what is transferred into the food, making it the tastiest and the loveliest meal ever. It is almost as if, when I am eating it, I am also absorbing her kindness and love towards me. All these emotions are reflected in the taste that satisfies not only my hunger but all my heart and soul.

In a restaurant, a chef may cook under pressure, for their love of cooking or sometimes, simply for the money. They may include technique and carefully chosen, quality ingredients, but they lack the special love and care that enhances the flavours of home food. That is why, no matter how good, one can simply not suffice on outside food.

Similarly, my dear reader, no matter what you do in life, do it with love, care and a positive attitude. For your thoughts and positive vibrations, reflect on your actions, and the more you put in, the better the results you will get. Do it for yourself.

Success does not simply depend on technique and skill, but your intentions behind your actions.

So, act with your whole heart and move forward. This way, the result won't just be your success but the feeling of happiness and content.

Which is your favorite dish made by your mother?

Chapter 7: A Boat

"A positive attitude causes a chain reaction of positive thoughts, events and outcomes. It is a catalyst and it sparks extraordinary results."

—Wade Boggs

People often tell me that their life feels a little too stressful, especially because of their habit of overthinking. Of how things would be so much better if they didn't digress into things and could just think like everyone else. To this I always wondered, is overthinking really such a bad habit? If one never digressed into a situation or an idea, then would anyone ever have discovered anything new? Not really, right? So overthinking cannot be all that bad.

I would like to consider it as a process of thinking deeper into a matter. Something that has the power to mess you up; but also has the power to reach beyond the ordinary and achieve something new and better. It may be a discovery, an epiphany or just a deeper understanding of society, spirituality or the journey towards one's own mental peace.

Exploring into different directions and entering new territory; all of it can be achieved and uncovered with the mind. The prowess of thinking.

As we discussed in the previous chapter, our thoughts are like codes used to create our own website. Each webpage, a compilation of our thoughts and ideas put together and assembled in an order that best represents us. While these thoughts are a part of our conscious mind, thinking in itself is a subconscious process. You might not always have control over your flow of thinking, but you are still the captain of your own thoughts. In fact, manoeuvring your thoughts is a lot like sailing.

While on a sailboat, travelling in the opposite direction of the wind is called windward sailing. Here, trimming the angle and shape of the sails by forming a familiar foil shape, creates a difference in pressure. This uses the wind blowing against the boat to push the boat perpendicular to the wind's direction.

This also requires observing the flow of the wind and understanding the change in its direction, while being aware of your surroundings.

Similarly, you need to be aware of the flow of your subconscious thoughts to accordingly adjust your narrative and conscious mind to your preferred direction. This may seem hard, but with patience and practice, you can enable yourself to guide your mind in directions that lead to new discoveries and achievements.

Therefore, overthinking is not good or bad, it is only a journey of your thoughts that need to be tilted in the right direction.

For this, meditate, it will help you be more aware of yourself; with every day it will feel easier and you will eventually be able to consciously channel your subconscious thoughts towards your preferred destination.

Note down your understanding of how you think and react to situations and reflect on it.

Life is an Art

Chapter 8: A Precious Painting

"The aim of art is to represent not the outward appearance of things, but their inward significance"

– Aristotle

You are a painter and your life is a canvas. The beauty of a painting depends on the selection of colours, designs and patterns used to create it. Each curve and line contributes to defining its shape. Though in reality, you cannot erase anything once it's drawn, you can keep modifying it to your taste by adding additional lines. You can also get creative by combining different colours. You see, there is no bad art, but if you still think you made a mistake, don't give up. Keep going because every piece has the scope of becoming a masterpiece.

This is the first painting of my two-year-old son. Initially, I thought of it as a simple, child's scribbling, but soon enough I realized that it's a very precious painting. Not just because it is my son's first painting, but because it single-handedly depicts my entire life.

For the first time ever, I got to see my whole life in a painting. Each colour represents different aspects of my life. Yet, somehow very complex to understand. When I see the full painting, I see no defined  structure, it is only when I zoom in and see a small part of it, that I see a single coloured straight line. Making me realize that when I look at my whole life with its past, present and future together, it feels overwhelmingly complex. But when I solely look at the present moment it is just a simple coloured straight line that has the possibility to fill me with happiness. This simple painting teaches you that you don't always have to look at the whole picture. Just like the painting, look to the present and it will always be straight and simple. Be happy with that and enjoy what you have, cause then each new line will make its own meaning just like each new problem will bring its own solution.

I have seen many paintings, some paintings can be easily understood while others seem very complex, some even require the painter themselves to explain the meaning of it. But from what I have noticed, complex paintings are usually more valuable. So don't mind if your painting is complex and people don't seem to understand it. Remember that not every person has the vision to understand your painting. Sometimes you may need to explain its meaning to the ones that matter.

Every painting has its meaning; you just need to develop that vision to uncover all hidden secrets.

So, this story reminds us,

- Be your unique self, sometimes people may not understand you. Don't mind it.

- The complexities of your life only make it more valuable.

- Your life is more precious than anything else in this universe, embrace it and take care of it.

- Don't be afraid to ask questions, never assume anything about others, it is better to clear the air than to live in doubt.

- Be the best painter of your precious painting of this universe.

Take any picture in your home and write down the meaning you see in it. How does it co-relate with your life?

Chapter 9: A Beautiful Garden

*"We may think we are nurturing
our garden, but of course it's our garden
that is really nurturing us"*

– Jenny Uglow

One day I went to my society garden with my little son. It is full of trees and flowers. My son loves playing there and I enjoy sitting on the bench and watching the flowers blossom. It gives me a certain peace of mind.

The gardener sows the seeds, gives them fertilizers, water and removes the weeds for better growth of the plants.

The more I observe, the easier it fits, one of the many different aspects of nurturing one's own life.

Your mind is the fertile soil, your thoughts and ideas, seeds. Every adversity that crosses your path in life makes you more robust, acting as a fertilizer and the negative thoughts as the unwanted weeds that grow in the garden. Whatever seed is sown in that soil will eventually grow. So choose the seeds you decide to nurture, weed out the bad ones and maintain your garden regularly. Use each adversity you run into as fertilizer to be more robust. Don't let your beautiful garden be polluted by other peoples toxicity and never forget to sit back and enjoy watching the flowers bloom.

This isn't just an inspirational vague metaphor, but an accurate and implementable analogy that can be made real by keeping certain factors in mind;

- **The Vision**

You have to actively sow the seeds you want to grow in your garden. You cannot sow just any seed you get. Visualize the type of garden you want. What kinds of flowers, vegetables and trees should grow there? The clearer idea you have the easier it gets to work for it. The same goes for your life. What type of life do you want for yourself? What is your goal? According to that, you then need to work forward and turn that vision into reality.

- **Fertile soil**

You need fertile soil to grow good plants and flowers in your garden. Gardeners spend so much time and energy to make it suitable for the better growth of plants. Similarly, you need to spend much time on your health, education, skill and personality development, to keep your mind and therefore your life, fertile. Healthy growth of plants is not possible without suitable and fertile soil, just as your growth is not possible without a progressive environment and skills required to achieve your goals.

- **Selection of seeds to sow**

It is the most important task for the Gardener. He knows that he has to reap what he sows. If he sows watermelon seeds, he reaps watermelons. Is it possible for him to sow watermelon seeds in order to procure muskmelons? Whatever you sow, will grow; it is very important to act with the purpose of achieving the desired results. Similarly, if you want to keep your family happy, you need to give them your time and attention instead of ignoring them and spending more time at work.

- **Prioritizing your goals**

You have limited space in your garden but you have a variety of seeds to sow in there. What do you do? You prioritize. You have many goals in your life but you cannot work on all of them at the same time. Trim this list down and focus on what is needed in your present moment.

Remember that you have put a lot of effort into your garden, and that alone makes it very special. The closer it is to your vision, the more time you will want to spend in it. But at the same time, if you don't acknowledge the little unexpected changes and adapt to them, you will never be able to appreciate what you have created. One simply cannot give their hundred per cent to something they don't appreciate. So work with everything life throws at you, use it to make your vision come true and give it all your love. Others will eventually come to appreciate it as much as you do.

Be the best gardener you can be for your beautiful garden. It is worth every bit of your effort.

What have you observed and learned during your garden visit?

Chapter 10: The Race

"It is important to understand the objective of every race. Sometimes it is important to win. Sometimes it is more than enough if you just complete the race."

— Abhishek Ratna

"Life is a race… If you don't run fast you will be like a broken anda…." one of the most powerful dialogues from the movie 3 idiots. But is it really true? Is only running enough to win?

A race could be any competition and in competition, our ultimate goal is to win. But what if we don't even know that we are a part of the said competition? Then what? Everyone thinks that a race can have only two ends; Winning or Losing. But what most people don't realise is that there is a third unnoticed and underrated end; No one cares about it though one could say that it is the most important one of them all. It is the experience and happiness that comes with participating. Remember that this third end is the most precious one of them all.

One simple car race between two friends teaches us a very precious lesson of life.

Two friends, Aarav and Darsh, decided to have a very odd car race with three conditions;

1. It would be held between two cities, with one being the starting point and the other being the finishing line.

2. One of them would use the new expressway that takes 90 minutes to cover the distance while the other would use the old highway which doubles the time to do the same.

3. A coin toss would decide which contestant takes which route.

Probably the only fair condition to this unfair game.

Once all the conditions were agreed upon and the date and time were finalised, the only thing left was the race itself.

On the main day, the coin toss decided that Aarav would take the expressway while Darsh would have to take the old highway, and as expected, Aarav won the race. He felt overjoyed, not just by the obvious win but because of the smooth expressway that allowed him to ease through at full speed. Even though he had thoroughly enjoyed his ride, he did feel bad for his friend who had to use the old route which wasn't just longer, but a lot less smooth. After a long wait of almost two whole hours, Darsh finally arrived. Aarav greeted him immediately, wanting to console him for the inevitable loss but saw no trace of frustration or a sense of loss on his face. Confused, he asked Darsh how he seemed so satisfied with the results and got a very simple yet meaningful answer in return.

Darsh replied, "Since I already knew that I was going to lose, I decided to focus on and enjoy the road instead. The villages and scenic routes that crossed my path and the people I got to encounter during my stops, really made the journey worth it. So even though I lost, I would not change a thing about it". And with that, they managed to achieve a fair ending to an incredibly unfair race.

Just like this one odd incident, our life too is a race. Some are privileged enough to get a headstart while for others it is a little unfair. So, instead of competing with the people around you, focus on your journey. You will realise that the only person you need to compete with is yourself.

Sometimes, you may feel like you have to reach your destination as fast as possible, but you are forgetting that it is the journey itself that guides you to your final destination. Would it even be possible to reach your goals without your experiences? The mistakes you learn from and the memories that fill you with joy and keep you strong in times of need. The people that you meet on your way and the people that leave midway. These are the things that actually matter.

So reader, not every race is about winning or losing. In certain races, like the one of life, it is the participation that counts and the results are the beautiful memories you hold. Embrace the sorrows and hardships coming into your life, keep moving forward and enjoy the journey. For you will soon realise it to be your true achievement in life.

Did you win or lose in your last competition? What did you learn from it?

____

____

____

____

____

____

____

Chapter 11: The River

"No man ever steps in the same river twice, for it's not the same river and he's not the same man."

– Heraclitus

A river has a continuous flow of water; it has life, a beautiful sound and movement in infinite variations. It is the vein of the earth as are veins in our body. A place that renews energy; connecting the past with the future and linking it all in the rhythm of its flow. It teaches us the precious lessons of life. You just need to change the way you see it, and to help you with that, I present to you a life-changing conversation between a father and son on the river bank.

There was once a small village that stood on the bank of a river. One morning, a father decided to take his 10-year-old son to swim in the river. It was a lovely day and the boy was jumping with excitement when they set off from home. After a short journey, they reached their destination and the father seated himself on a rock near the water, silently watching the flow of the river. Confused by his father's actions, the boy decided to stand and wait next to him. Hours passed by and the boy started losing his patience but his father did not budge. Finally infuriated, the son snapped, "Father, why would you get me here for a swim if all you wanted to do was sit and stare at the river?"

To this, the father replied, as calmly as ever, "Son, you see, the water in this river is a little dirty. I am simply waiting for the flow of water to stop so that all the dirt can settle down and the water can be clean enough to swim in".

This reply angered the son even more, "NOTHING CAN STOP THE FLOW OF A RIVER", he shouted feeling like he was being ridiculed.

To this, the father started laughing, "that's the point, isn't it?".

Upon seeing his son's confused face he continued, "Son you are growing up and before you know it, you will be taking up a lot of responsibilities. I brought you here at the river bed, not to have you swim in this river but to teach you how to swim in the river of life. You see, this river represents life itself and its flow represents all of time. The flow of time doesn't stop for anyone, no matter how many obstacles come your way. If you stop and wait for your problems to disappear, you'll never get to live and enjoy your life. You will never reach your desired destination if you're stuck waiting for things to settle down. So instead, dive into the river and keep swimming, face your obstacles and make your route. The flow will guide you and eventually, you will reach your desired destination.

There is no right time for anything, so give your best no matter what and every moment will become the right moment for you.

With this, both the father and the son dive into the river and seized the blissful day.

Have you ever visited a river? What does it signify to you?

____

____

____

____

____

____

____

____

Chapter 12: A Rose

"If a rose is full of thorns, it does not mean it's not full of beauty."

– Matshona Dhliwayo

What is your opinion of yourself? If someone accused you of being a bad person, you would probably accept it. But if someone came and complimented you, how would you react to that? Accept the compliment? Or underplay your own self as a form of resistance?

Many times, you may feel like you are not good enough. Finding it much easier to love and appreciate others, than to love yourself. But where does this lack of self-love come from?

How did we go from being a tiny baby that knows nothing of perfection or the struggles of life to becoming people who drown in their own problems and constantly feel unworthy or unlovable to some degree or another? What happened?

Think about a rose, from the time it is a tiny bud to the moment its last petal falls. It keeps changing from one stage to another, yet, it is always beautiful at every stage. It is full of thorns and still remains a desired symbol of love. Never have the thorns stopped anyone from appreciating the roses.

You are no different. You are and always have been perfect and beautiful at every stage of life. You are doing the best you can with the knowledge, awareness and understanding you have. As you gain more knowledge, understand better and become more aware, you start to do things differently. That is just how learning works, it is a continuous process.

We are always searching for beauty outside but in reality, it is hidden within us. In your life, you developed a habit of concentrating on the thorns. Change it. Concentrate on the beauty of the rose that you are instead and notice how life changes for the better.

You may face many adversities in the process but that doesn't make you any less beautiful and lovable, just like a rose. The thorns protect the rose the way your adversities give you the experience to be robust and protect yourself.

Here are some simple steps to help you fall in love with yourself:

- Spend more time in your own company and in activities that bring you joy.

- Be kind to yourself.

- Leave all of the negative thoughts you have

about yourself, and try to see yourself in a more positive light.

- Don't try to be perfect, remember that nothing is perfect in this world.

- Know your worth; weaknesses and strengths- it will help you to accept yourself better.

- Be honest with yourself and accept that you are a beautiful rose.

- Develop the habit of gratitude and forgiveness- It will help you ease all of your sufferings.

- Pen down your life story- it may inspire others.

- Love yourself, accept the thorns of life and be happy.

Which is your favorite flower? What can you learn from it?

Chapter 13: A Baby

"Children see magic because they look for it."

– Christopher Moore

My little son is almost two years old. He does not have to do anything to be perfect. He knows that he is the centre of the universe and everyone loves him. He has a big smile on his face whenever he looks at himself in the mirror, loves all his body parts and isn't ever afraid to ask questions. He knows that he can get whatever he wants, even if it is by crying. The entire neighbourhood might know that he is angry, but they also know when he is happy and how his smile lights up every room. So full of love and happiness, he is the definition of a perfectly content being.

We too used to be the same when we were babies. We were perfect, everyone around us loved us, we loved all our body parts and we smiled when we saw ourselves in the mirror.

But with time, we grew up and all of that changed. Our beliefs changed, we were not 'perfect' anymore. We couldn't love ourselves the same, couldn't smile at our reflections the same. But where did these new ideas and beliefs come from?

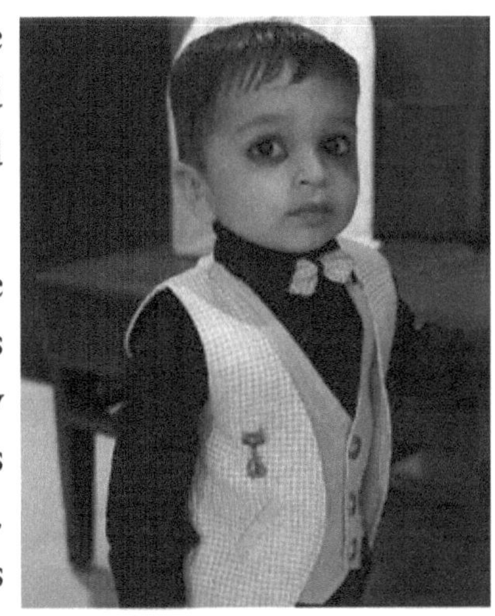

Well, they came from the elders around us. They taught us that life is very complicated. They taught us 'the customs of the world'. What one can do and what one cannot. What one should do and what one should not. In short, our minds were polluted by society.

To follow all of its norms and beliefs, we killed the baby within us and kept trying to search for love and perfection from other sources. Trying to live up to an unnatural standard.

We need not search for any of it outside; we just need to wake the baby sleeping within us. When that baby awakens; our life will be lovable and perfect again.

Simple steps to wake up the baby sleeping inside you,

- Appreciate each moment

- Don't take tension- Stressing over everything won't give you any solution

- Smile at yourself whenever you look into the mirror

- Dreamlike a baby and do your best to achieve it all

- Love all your body parts and respect yourself

- Love and give respect to all the people around you without judgment.

- Believe in yourself. You are the centre of your universe.

Do you have any memories from when you were a baby? What do you cherish the most?

____

____

____

____

____

____

____

Chapter 14: Book & Pen

Life is like a pen, with you as the writer. Writing your life story in a big fat book, that is the world.

Your every move, every decision- your success and your failures. Everything you do gets recorded in this book. Your footsteps doused in ink layout your prints for the future generations to follow.

Don't you want to leave prints worth following? To write a book that motivates and inspires the future generation.

So, what are you doing to make this happen? Are you considerate of what you're writing? Have you ever revisited old pages to review your work? And most of all,

Are you satisfied with it?

When you were born you held a fresh pen with this world, still a fresh book. You started using your precious pen's ink. Filling up page after page. So many pages, so much ink—scribbling through like nothing matters. But this is where you are incorrect you see, a lot of it matters. Being a writer may come with a lot of creative freedom, but you tend to forget that the pages in themselves are finite. The world may be a big, fat book, but there are only so many pages for you to fill, only so much ink for you to use.

To top that, there is your pen. It's more like an old fountain pen, beautiful to write with but can be really messy at times, has a lot of chances of spilling and may break, if not treated well.

Who knows what will happen tomorrow.

One thing you need to know is that the ink in your pen and the pages of your book keep reducing by the day. Suddenly, one day you may realise that you have wasted your time scribbling through your precious pages and frantically try to write something better. But it feels too late now. You don't know what would make things better. You had never really given it an actual thought before this. And now what? Pretty soon it will all be over and all you'll be left with is a heart filled with regret over a life half lived.

Well, that's not true though. One good thing about life is that as long as you breathe, it's never too late.

Start now, use your ink and these pages with care. Write each word keeping in mind that each drop of ink writes YOUR story. Don't waste a single drop on anything unworthy. If your pen breaks down in between you should be satisfied with whatever you have written up to that very moment.

Live each moment with happiness for you don't know what will happen next. Live like every moment is the last moment of your life and write each word like it will be the last word of your story.

Life is too short to simply scribble your way through. Live, love and grow, write your story in a way that your every word may inspire the next one.

Do you ever think about your life story? Write about any important event from your life that you find inspiring.

____

____

____

____

____

____

____

Chapter 15: Seasons

There are four to six seasons in a year, depending on where you live. Namely, the three major ones from where I come from would be Winter, Summer and Monsoon.

We usually plan and prepare for seasons beforehand, purchasing all that is necessary for us to be able to enjoy every bit of it without being affected by the drastic weather changes they bring with them.

One such monsoon day, I sat on my chair and thought, "What if our life was like a year?"

It too has different seasons or rather, stages starting from infancy to death, with the three major ones being childhood, adulthood and old age.

How do you see your life; do you appreciate each stage the way you appreciate each season? Or have you already picked favourites? The way students love the summers and farmers love the monsoons, have you already chosen your childhood?

Childhood, the best and most innocent part of life, the mind is still not polluted with old beliefs, responsibilities, insecurities and the pressure of living up to the expectations of others. Children have so many dreams they want to fulfil but, once we hit adulthood, most of these dreams slowly take a backseat, eventually getting crushed under the burden of our new responsibilities and the pressure of satisfying the people in our life.

You now have to secure a family, their wellbeing, and your old age. All by yourself.

It is in your human nature to never be satisfied. You are busy worrying about something or the other. You no longer have the time to think of your childhood dreams, your wishes or your hobbies. It's almost as if you spend your entire adulthood simply preparing for old age. And your old age, preparing for death itself, praying to god and hoping for a new life to start and live better.

But you see, that would be like spending the entirety of your summer just preparing for monsoons and then the monsoons for the coming winter and so on. Sounds ridiculously pointless, doesn't it?

Remember that time does not stop for anybody. When you reach old age, you regret not enjoying your adulthood. What is the point of earning so much money if you can no longer even spend it on what you've wanted all your life? There are so many dreams that you simply cannot fulfil once you hit old age. So why do you choose to live a life half lived? Try to enjoy every moment as you would all seasons. They are all there for a reason and are equally important in your life.

Adulthood is a precious time that works as a bridge between your childhood and old age. It is the time to fulfil your dreams and to create memories that you can smile back at in your old age. It is the stories you tell your children and the adventures that bring you all the best treasures of life.

Therefore my reader, enjoy each moment of your life like it is the last moment you will ever live. Live life like a child; spend some time fulfilling your own wishes that give you happiness and some to fulfil your responsibility which promises you stability. For, it is only your happiness that you spread to your loved ones.

Write down any one of your childhood dreams. Have you completed it yet? What is a memory you would take to your old age?

Chapter 16: The Traffic Signal

"I wish life had traffic lights, it would tell us when to go for it, when to be careful, and when to just stop"

– Anurag Prakash Ray

Life is short and everyone is hustling. Moving so fast, one can barely comprehend their own actions. But have you ever considered what exactly fuels this hustle? It is our sense of competition, our need to win and our compulsive habit of comparing ourselves to others.

More often than you realise, you end up comparing yourself to those who are richer and more successful than you are, and it is all good as long as it drives you to do better in life. But what about the times you start feeling insecure? When you suddenly feel so inferior that you don't know what to do.

One day, a few years ago, I had an experience that truly made me aware of this little phenomenon. I was on my way to a friend's house; waiting for a traffic signal to turn green when I noticed the most beautiful car in front of me. It was the latest model of the BMW that had recently been released. We had just stopped at the signal when I noticed it. It was a beautiful black BMW driven by a man around the same age as I was. At that moment, I couldn't help but compare that beautiful car to my average little scooter and I cannot express how inferior I suddenly felt. I was so lost in my insecurity when; as if out of thin air, a beggar appeared next to me, asking for some money. I was abruptly brought back to reality and without even thinking, I loosely muttered, "Well at least I'm better than this guy" as I reached into my pocket to give him some change. It was only a few moments later as the signal finally turned green that it hit me. I no longer felt bad about my scooter. I may not have had the latest version of the BMW but I was still privileged enough to live a comfortable life. I was grateful.

You see, it is simply a part of our human nature to compare, we feel inferior when we see something, we believe to be better than us and superior when that something seems to be beneath us.

Remember that if you are reading this, you are richer than at least 68.8 % of the population of India. That in itself is a privilege and achievement. Now all you have to do is grow. Give your best no matter what you do. If you can think of it, you can achieve it. Your future is in your hands. With hard work and dedication, the biggest failure can be turned into success. Just like the story of the hare and the tortoise, you get to choose your own outcome.

Comparing yourself to others may not always give you happiness. Don't compare yourself with anyone, everyone is different and we all have our unique value; you cannot compare the moon to the sun.

So, embrace your life and whatever you have, work towards growth and enjoy each moment with happiness.

Write your own experience on a traffic signal.

Let go

Chapter 17: The Tree

> *"Letting go means to come to the realization that some people are a part of your history, but not a part of your destiny."*
>
> *– Steve Maraboli*

All the wisdom is stored in the trees, you just need to figure out how to understand them. The oldest tree known to man is The Great Basin Bristlecone Pine, with its age of over Five Thousand Years. On average, trees need over a decade to simply grow from a sapling and can live for almost and over a century in all their glory. This comes from their ability to adapt and grow within their surroundings and also, despite them. Something very important for us to learn as people as well. Nothing in life is permanent. There will always be ups and downs in your life. Your success and happiness only depend on how you cope with, and despite the situations at hand.

- **The Autumn**

Every evening while walking home, I took this path that had this beautiful tree on it. Every day I made sure to pass through so I would never miss it. It was a big, magnificent Gulmohar tree with an infinite number of leaves and beautiful red flowers that looked like they kept all the secrets of the world hidden within them. So high and mighty, it felt like it could be the lone protector of our world. Then one day, suddenly, autumn arrived. I remember that evening very well. My beautiful tree had lost all its flowers and almost all its leaves. Like it had lost a war, it looked like a skeleton without a soul, a warrior with his armour shattered; the dried-up yellow fallen leaves were like its remnants scattered all around it. Yet, the warrior stood strong, keeping itself together, waiting to blossom again.

And blossom it did. It took its time but one day while walking, I finally noticed a few small but beautiful leaves growing back as if peeking out to see if it was okay to come out. It was only a matter of weeks after that; the tree bloomed again, filled with leaves and beautiful red flowers, somehow looking more glorious than ever.

This got me thinking, even though it felt so gloomy to see the tree lose all its leaves, if that hadn't happened, it would never have gotten the new ones and turned into the version it is today. This tree lost all its leaves every autumn season and stood strong till new leaves and flowers bloomed again. So if you're losing something, it's probably time to let go. And if it is time, then one should stand strong and keep going, for it will soon be time for something better to come along and take its place. Consider it your personal autumn season and keep hope. Enjoy every moment and as cliché, as it may sound, remember, that everything happens for a reason.

- **The Bark**

The picture attached below is of the dried up bark of a shedding tree. I know this because I am the one who clicked it. Turns out, this phenomenon occurs every year as well, a tree shedding its dry outer bark to preserve itself. Did you know? A similar phenomenon also occurs within our bodies. Every seven to ten years, all the cells in our body die and get replaced by new ones. Therefore, within a span of a decade, you are a whole new human being. At least physically speaking, mentally; it may be a little harder for us human beings to move on and let go of the people we were and the things that happened in our life. And it is mainly the bad memories, isn't it? The ones who left you, how they hurt you and what you went through. The good ones are usually overpowered and more likely forgotten, making the world feel like a harder place to live in.

But dear reader, if the tree can shed its old bark, and your cells can replace themselves, then you too can surely try to replace the budding hate from your past with the new hope of a bright future.

Why stick to the past when change is all we see, day after day, year after year, seasons, technology and even other people.

The world is as you perceive it, so look at this world like it may as well be heaven, let go of the beliefs that are holding you back. Be a new person every year; evolve not just physically, but mentally as well.

Have you ever planted any trees? Write down your experience with it.

Importance of Adversity

Chapter 18: The Curry

"Pressure can burst a pipe, or pressure can make a diamond."

– Robert Horry

Vegetables, spice and water are the main ingredients for a curry. But simply throwing them together in a pot does not do the trick; your ingredients need to be cooked. It takes applying a certain amount of heat and pressure (dum) to these ingredients—for a particular period of time, based on their proportions—to complete the dish.

Now if one would compare life to a curry. The different ingredients would be us, the people and places we surround ourselves with, our beliefs and natural circumstances, etcetera. Like any good curry, life too requires fine ingredients, but that isn't sufficient. For cooking, a certain amount of heat and dum is required to complete the dish. This heat and dum comes in the form of the obstacles we face in life—our bad experiences, heartbreaks, losses and stressors. These are the things we learn from and grow.

But what happens when the pressure is too much?

The dish starts to fall apart. Such stress may lead to chronic anxiety and depression.

Sounds scary, right? But that doesn't mean we give up on cooking. Good food indeed leads to a good life, and a good life just like good food requires patience and heedfulness.

Depression and anxiety are very common diseases in today's time and can affect any and all age groups. According to a 2017 study from 'Our World In Data'; a project by Global Change Data Lab, around 10.7% of the world's population faces some or the other mental health disorder, which comes to a whopping number of 792 million people globally. With around 264 million (3.4%) and 284 million (3.85%) suffering from depression and anxiety disorders, respectively.

You may feel utterly overwhelmed at many points in your life. This may be due to heavy workload, family or relationship problems and even set, unattainable expectations.

Think of these obstacles and stressors not as impossible and depressing; but as the heat and dum required to complete your dish.

Patiently observe this process of the making of your curry and try to grasp the importance of the obstacles coming into your life. Keep tasting your dish while cooking it, see what goes well and what doesn't, how much heat and dum is enough and what is too much. Not all the existing recipes are meant for you, so choose for yourself.

Take every stressor and obstacle positively and find an outlet to release the pressure built in your life. The chapter on the tiny cotton plant in this book will help you to identify the outlets to release this stress and pressure.

"Curry is a mixture of vegetables and spices, both are required to make it tasty; Life is a mixture of happiness and sorrows, both are required to make a successful life"

Which is your favorite curry? How do you personalise it to your taste?

____

____

____

____

____

____

____

Chapter 19: Water

"A drop of water, if it could write out its own history, would explain the universe to us."

– Lucy Larcom

If rivers are the veins then water is the blood flowing through our planet. It is the most important element for our planet and life. Over 70% of the earth is covered with water and over 70% of our body is also composed of water. This is not a coincidence.

Water is the centrepiece of our universe. It is a liquid. Taking the shape of any vessel you pour it in, it evaporates into steam under intense heat, turns to ice when it's cold enough to freeze and eventually condenses back into its true form, as and when required. Persistent flow of water cuts through rocks and boulders crossing its path. Water is strong enough to create, shelter and destroy life, all by itself—making it vital for everything that lives. A rainbow is formed on the gloomiest of days when sunlight is refracted by passing through droplets of water and with the same light, that single drop of water can show you a reflection of your entire life.

You are very much like water. You are the centrepiece. You have all the qualities and capabilities of water. You start just as pure and mould just as easily to your surroundings. You may be constricted to the flow of time but you also have the power to create and destroy on the way. So if obstacles come your way, be persistent and cut them down. Make your own path and reach your destination.

There is so much that you have experienced and so much more to go. At times you might evaporate due to the heat of your own anger and frustrations and freeze under the stone-cold pain of sorrows and loss. You might feel like you're something you never wanted to be or that you're stuck with no motivation to move forward, but with time you will always turn back into water. A peaceful, refined version of yourself.

Trust in yourself, Hope is the light you use to make a rainbow on a gloomy day. You reflect, the lives you see and evolve as you grow.

Be it and believe in it. Do not restrict yourself to a glass, a river or even the sea. You get to hone your skills, grow and make your own destiny. You can be as calm as the ocean and as strong as the tides, as chaotic as waves and flow as steady as the currents. You have the power to be infinite and yet manage to be contained. Therefore, build your nature, give life meaning, help others flourish and never forget that you are the most important element there can be.

What do you think about water?

Chapter 20: The Mysterious Highway

"Life is a highway - the enjoyment you get depends on the lane you choose"

– Joel Fuhrman

'Driving' on the highway of life is simply about steadily moving forward in your lane. A deeper meaning of your life is hidden in this regular highway that you may drive on daily. Have you ever attempted to uncover it? Well, it is a rather simple one, but it really helps change the way you look at the struggles of life. It is something I realised when I was driving on the state highway during one of my journeys.

I was driving to another town for my college reunion. The event was for Monday afternoon but I decided to leave the night before since I knew the roads very well and it would give me time to get some rest and go in fresh.

I was very excited to meet my old friends and classmates and was reminiscing about old times when I was abruptly pulled back by what I could only assume to be a really huge pothole. I slowed down my car, in my excitement, I had forgotten how much I hated this particular road and how over time its condition had only gotten worse. I was suddenly very frustrated now. I cursed the government and the politicians for not maintaining the highway; feeling helpless and annoyed. I mean a good 3km stretch completely ragged, the highway in itself so ill-maintained, it was only after a good 15 minutes of uncomfortable driving when the road became favourable again. I finally accelerated the speed and completed the next 50kms within an easy 30-40 minutes. I finally got to my hotel where I instantly fell asleep. The next morning I had completely forgotten about the frustration of my drive. It was no more than a story I was to tell about my journey accompanied by a few comments on the road and the government. As I got to the reunion and met everybody, I thought to myself, what if I had stopped on that pothole and turned around? I would have never reached my destination and returned home frustrated. I would have missed this beautiful and wholesome experience.

It may sound oversimplified, but our life's journey is a lot like this highway. In fact, we pass a lot of such highways throughout. One minute you are delighted with your smooth, easy-going life and the other you bump into seemingly unending potholes, speed breakers and ridiculous traffic that make you want to just stop and turn around. But just like my story, you cannot let a bad road stop you from getting to your destination.

Our journeys will never be smooth all the time; there will always be obstacles, some frustrating, others nerve-wracking and some disappointingly depressing. In that case, it is okay to slow down and break your pace on your expectations of happiness and success. You may be criticized by the people around you, but they are not driving on your road, are they? Keep driving forward in your efforts to face your problems, solve the ones you can and move on from the ones you cannot. Eventually, those difficult times will pass and soon enough everything will seem right again. If you stop and wait for the problems to solve themselves, you might get stuck within those hurdles for a lifetime.

Always remember that once you reach your destination, you will eventually forget about the bad road, thinking of it simply as the tale of your journey. Try to face these hurdles with a smile, keep your spirits high and you will reach your destination on time.

Life in itself is a mysterious highway, and your future depends on how you choose to face your journey. Face it with a smile.

Do you drive? Pen down your experience of a bad road and how would you correlate it with your life.

Chapter 21: A Precious Stone

– Michelangelo

The value of a stone depends on its quality and usefulness. Did you know that you are also like a stone? Your Value is also very much dependent on your quality and usefulness. Don't get me wrong, your self-worth is immeasurable to no doubt.

But, just hear me out here.

I have been seeing a big stone on my way to the office for many years. It is an enormous stone, but I don't think that anybody has ever really noticed it. It is too big to carry and most likely of no use. What is the value of it being there for hundreds of years? What is its purpose? I always wonder.

Similarly, you might be beautiful or strong or very rich and powerful. But what is your value if you are not useful to your society? If there is nobody to care, to learn from you or to spread your values. Nobody who you can relate to or who can relate to you? You are just sitting alone in one corner of the world, just existing.

In your journey, you may face situations that break you down, people that cause you pain and times where you have to find your way. These seemingly awful things are what really enhance your value. Just like a stone. Whether it is granite, marble, onyx, alabaster or a diamond, they are as good as useless when they aren't discovered, broken down, sculpted or polished. They are just there, very much like the stone near my office. You see, your adversities break you down and in the process; you are sculpted and polished to your true value.

Let us look back to that big stone, what happens when someone finds it and breaks it down? People can now carry it and use it for construction and other purposes, one can figure out its true value only after its discovery.

Some may say that it might lose its majestic nature, but one may never truly know.

A sculptor may hit his hammer on it and turn it into a masterpiece; maybe it would be worshipped as an idol or kept in a showroom. The stone is the same, but now its values increased. Of course, this doesn't mean that you could become a god, but you definitely have the potential to become somebody's inspiration or mentor. Somebody who teaches as well as learns and gives back as much as they take. This process doesn't just give your life value, but also makes it a beautiful one to live in.

Similarly, once you get out there, you too may find a sculptor who discovers you and guides you to become a masterpiece in yourself. You may have to bear the pain of hammering, but in the end, it will be way better than sitting undiscovered in a corner. So consider life, and everyone who you meet in your journey a sculptor for you, never know the value of the hidden jewel you are inside.

The pain and trouble will uncover your hidden talent, make you stronger and cultivate your true value. Soon it will open doors for you that you had never noticed or expected before.

You have the potential to climb the mountain of success and happiness and to be a sculptor yourself.

In that my dear stone, rests your true value, and all you need to do is be brave and get out there so you can be discovered.

What is the most valuable stone in your life?

Chapter 22: Monsoons

"Life isn't about waiting for the storm to pass…
It's about learning to dance in the rain."

– Vivian Greene

It was monsoon season. I was only 10 years old when I witnessed my first proper thunderstorm. That day, there was no light at home because of the power cut caused by non-stop rain. The winds were blowing aggressively, a sky full of dark clouds, with the only occasional light being of the lightning followed by the nerve-wracking sound of thunder. It was absolutely terrifying. That was the first of many stormy days that were spent that season, the other days seemed rather dull in comparison really. Since then, it was always raining, always gloomy and we were never allowed to go out and play. We only went to school and then straight back home. When we complained, we were told that if we got wet and dirty, we would get sick. That is how most of the monsoon was spent, boring, and indoors. It was so sad, I almost felt like it would never end, well, until it did. And suddenly it all felt worth it. It was around the end of monsoon season, and I was finally allowed to go out and play. It had rained the previous night but the sky had been clear all day. The weather was really beautiful now and the atmosphere felt lighter, everything seemed greener than usual and there was an earthy fragrance in the air. Even the grownups seemed happier; it was as if a spell was lifted from our planet.

It was only years later that I understood, the rains weren't the spell that was lifted, but the spell that created this rich atmosphere.

The same happens in your life too. Just like the monsoons, you may face times that feel absolutely gloomy and sad. There might be stormy days that feel frightening and create pure havoc in your life, and days on end where you cannot even leave home. Such times that feel completely wrong are unfortunately inevitable, no matter who you are and what you do. You may complain to God and the people around you and curse everything for the problems you face. But, just like the season of monsoon, these times too, are not as never-ending as they seem. The gloominess does eventually end and once the sky clears, it is almost like a spell that has been lifted. You may not really understand when it ends, but when you go outside you will realise the change.

Your head will feel clearer, the mood a little lighter and your world will feel greener than usual. Like the world was starting again.

All successful people face failure, loss and suffering. In fact, it is due to these struggles that they find their path to success.

"There is no birth of consciousness without pain." ~ Carl Jung

"One cannot get through life without pain… What we can do is choose how to use the pain life presents to us." ~ Bernie Siegel

"Learning is not child's play; we cannot learn without pain." ~ Aristotle

These are a few quotes said by writers and philosophers of different times and they all lead to one simple answer, it is our suffering that leads us to the meaning of our life. And it is this meaning that we derive that guides us towards our final destination, whatever it may be.

You create your future and your past is what you remember of it. Let's not forget that we cannot make curry without dum or the heat of the flames. Never lose hope, even if it feels like the end of the world. Dare to face it with everything that you feel, for whether you are stuck at home during the monsoons or withering like a tree during autumn, you will blossom again. Time doesn't stop for anyone, therefore everything has to pass eventually. No matter how good or bad.

Cherish every bit of it, live every moment to its fullest. Sadness is inevitable, depression is hard to escape, but every experience is unique. So live and learn through it all and eventually, things won't feel as awful anymore. And you will be content.

Pen down one of your best and worst experiences of the monsoons. How do they make you feel now?

Find the Solution

Chapter 23: Tiny Cotton Plant

"Energy and persistence conquers all things"

– Benjamin Franklin

We have already spoken about how one cannot achieve success or happiness without enduring any pain from the obstacles and stressors of life. The taste and quality of curry depend on the proportions and blends of its ingredients. Likewise, the proportions and blends of the people you surround yourself with, your actions and reactions with regards to the good and bad situations in your life, matter for your success. Even a pressure cooker needs an outlet to give way to excess steam, or else it will blast, and just like that, you too need to identify an outlet to release all the extra stress, to not blast and balance the taste of life.

One day at work, my colleagues and I were discussing mental health. Being from the pharmaceutical field, we have been no strangers to the concept of antidepressants and antianxiety medication or how widely they are sold. But knowing medicine, we are also aware of their limitations.

So the question was what would be a better alternative to overcome problems. It was an intense conversation and  a lot of opinions were shared, but the two ways that everybody agreed on were regular exercise and meditation.

- **Exercise** helps by reducing the levels of stress hormones like adrenaline and cortisol produced in the body. It also stimulates the production of endorphins which are natural painkillers and mood elevators.

- **Meditation** relaxes your muscles and induces a state of peacefulness in the mind. When meditating, one needs to focus and eliminate the jumbled stream of thoughts from their mind. This helps get in touch with one's consciousness and escape the stressors that cause depression.

But it is not very easy to adopt these practices in your daily life, is it? It is easier to adapt to bad habits as compared to the ones that are good for you. This is because bad habits give you instant gratification that is the immediate sense of pleasure and happiness, while good habits take time to show results and require more patience. This lack of patience makes it harder for us to inculcate good habits.

My father is a farmer and cotton is one of the main plants that he grows in his farm. The picture used above is of a small cotton plant he had sown.

He once told me that when he is sowing a seed, he is also visualising the cotton that is going to come out of it. He then puts all his effort and care into manifesting that image into reality. That way, even when he faces setbacks like dryness or pests, he never loses hope. He knows that with the right fertilizers, skill, proper care and continuous effort, he can get a good crop.

Those wise words from my father are valid for everything we do in life.

Anything you might start is going to be difficult the first time, but it gets progressively easier with practice and time. And then eventually, with enough practice, it turns into a skill that is easier to do than to avoid. It is said that it takes around 21 days to develop a habit, for it always takes time for our mind and body to get the hang of things.

So try to visualise the results when you are trying to adopt a new habit, take time to work on it regularly and slowly it will become a small plant and then into a fine crop that you can be proud of.

Remember the quote by Napoleon Hill- "Patience, persistence, and perspiration make an unbeatable combination for success"

List out your good habits and mention what efforts you had to put in to inculcate them.

____

____

____

____

____

____

____

Chapter 24: Lock & Key

– J. A. Konrath

One day I was visiting a close friend of mine at his place. We spoke for a while and as the conversation progressed, he started telling me about his problems. I could recognise that he was very troubled and visibly upset. He further explained to me how he kept trying to figure things out but somehow the more he tried to solve his issues, the more his situation worsened. I really empathised with him and wished I could help him out, but in the end, I was aware that there was very little that I could do for him. As the conversation went on, I decided to offer some advice. I told him that I understood his situation and that maybe he could try changing his approach towards finding a solution; you see, everybody has problems, none of which is bigger or smaller than the other. They are all very complicated and overwhelming. So sometimes the best approach is to look at your problems like separate, literal problems, maybe even from a third-person perspective, and to then look at one's resources to try and find the best possible solution for each one of them.

Of course, it is more complicated to work on and so he wasn't very pleased with what I had to say. He suddenly got very angry and bitterly spat out that I just wouldn't understand and that it simply wasn't that easy. I understood that this wasn't the best way to help him and was about to dismiss the conversation when I realised that he wasn't done. We had been really good friends since we were young and I could see that he needed some kind of relief from all the tension that had built up. I then decided on a different approach.

I asked him, "Hypothetically speaking, if a part of your house caught fire, what would you do?" He looked at me confused but reluctantly replied that he would extinguish it with water. I then asked him what if it was an electrical fire caused by a power fuse or faulty appliance or a kitchen fire. In that case, using water would only make it worse.

He still looked confused but was now a little curious and open to conversation. I took that as a sign to go ahead and asked him to give me two locks with their respective keys. He did as I said and got me what I asked for, still very curious and confused as to where I was going with this. I took the items with a smile and used the keys to shut both the locks. I then proceeded to purposely try and open the locks with the wrong key. He had been watching me the whole time and now spoke up sounding quite annoyed, "What exactly are you doing? Are you trying to break the lock or something?" I didn't directly respond but instead asked him if he knew who made the keys. Even more puzzled and a little frustrated he stated the obvious that the key came with the locks and thus was made by the same person who made the locks.

"Exactly!", I exclaimed, "So you agree that every lock comes with a key?". He nodded in annoyance but let me continue anyway.

You see, just like every lock has a key, every problem also has a solution. Sometimes, we are too emotionally invested to figure it out but if we try to step back and identify the problem, we will eventually find the right solution.

Similarly, if we panic and pour water on an electrical fire, it will definitely make it worse, but if we figure out what is causing the fire and shut down the appliance, we can eventually fix the whole problem, and even save ourselves from any further short circuits.

If anything, we are lucky our life is more like the lock than the fire, for we get to keep trying till we can find the right solution. And the more we understand that, the easier it is to keep calm and help ourselves better.

So my dear troubled friend, look at your problem again, but this time, not as a fire burning down your home but as the lock that just needs its right key.

How to solve the problem:

1) Identify the problem.

2) Figure out where you stand in the situation.

3) Identify the cause of this problem.

4) Make a list of different approaches to solve it

5) Identify the pros and cons of each approach

6) select the best approach as per your understanding,

7) Implement it and monitor progress

8) Check if your problem is solved

*If yes then way to go!!!

* If not

9) Go back to step 6

You will eventually get there.

Note down one of your problems with a strategy to solve it.

The Balance Sheet

According to Investopedia, «A balance sheet is a financial statement that provides a snapshot of what a company owns and owes, as well as the amount invested by shareholders.» It is released at the end of every financial year and helps calculate their profits and losses for the year. Based on these calculations, the company then understands the quality of their performance; compares their assets with their liabilities, and strategizes to prepare for the next financial year.

One more important aspect of the working of a company is an investment. Investment is putting in a company's capital, with the intention of making a profit. It plays a major role in the growth and value of a company, one miscalculation can lead to a huge loss, and yet there is no growth without it.

Have you ever thought of preparing a balance sheet for yourself? Not just for your monetary transactions, but one to keep a record of your growth in life.

While the balance sheet of a company looks at numbers, the balance sheet of life contains an account of your experiences, relationships, actions and your health. It helps you understand and predict your investments, priorities and priorities in future investments.

By preparing a sheet you can calculate your debts; in favours and relationships and prepare for your future actions regarding them. It might feel better to not know, to avoid regret and panic. But it is always better to know than to be caught off-guard, isn't it? After all, it is your past that you are reviewing, something that is done and dusted, that you can learn from and create options for yourself to do better.

Identify the area in which you have losses. Make a plan and ensure that it is not repeated.

Identify the area in which you've made a profit. Ensure to repeat it.

Make a plan for investment in that core area that helps you bring in profits and work on it.

Remember that a balance sheet is a crucial element for the growth of companies as well as your life. You need to monitor it from time to time.

Just ensure that your company should not be closed in debt.

Prepare yourself a balance sheet for the past 3 months.

Profit	Loss

Balance: Profit/ Loss

"Every balance sheet of life contains two columns, profit and loss"

"Your balance sheet of life will never get tallied, if your assets side is short of self-love and satisfaction"